SURA'S

ALICE IN W

A

OTHER STORIES

By
Neela Subramaniam

YOUNG KIDS PRESS
(An imprint of Sura College of Competition)
Chennai

© PUBLISHERS

ALICE IN WONDERLAND AND OTHER STORIES
by Neela Subramaniam

This Edition : July, 2023
Size : 1/8 Crown
Pages : 80

ISBN : 81-7478-808-5
Code : PG 1

YOUNG KIDS PRESS
[An imprint of Sura College of Competition]

Head Office: 1620, 'J' Block, 16th Main Road, Anna Nagar,
Chennai - 600 040. Phones: 044-48629977, 42043273.

Printed at Padmavathi Offset, Chennai - 600 032 and Published by
V.V.K.Subburaj for Young Kids Press [An imprint of Sura College of Competition]
1620, 'J' Block, 16th Main Road, Anna Nagar, Chennai - 600 040.
Phone: 48629977
e-mail: enquiry@surabooks.com; suracollege@gmail.com
website: www.surabooks.com

07 23 500

Contents

Page

1. Alice in Wonderland 1

2. The Flying Trunk 9

3. Puss in Boots 17

4. The Brave Little Tailor 25

5. The Emperor's New Clothes 35

6. Snow-White and Rose-Red 43

7. The Wild Swans 51

8. Rapunzel 61

9. Beauty and the Beast 69

A

One day in summer, a small girl called Alice, went for a walk in the wood near her house with her sister. Alice's sister sat down and began reading a book. Alice became very bored as there was nothing to do. She also felt very sleepy.

Suddenly, she saw a rabbit, who was dressed in a suit, running past her. It took out a watch from its waistcoat pocket and looked at it.

"Oh dear me! I'm going to be late again!" it said and began running.

Alice felt curious and decided to go after the rabbit. She jumped to her feet and followed it through the wood.

Alice saw the rabbit go down a large rabbit hole. She followed it at once down the tunnel. The rabbit hole went on like a dark tunnel for some time. Then suddenly Alice felt herself falling down, down down!

She landed with a thump on a pile of leaves. Alice walked down the passage and saw many doors. But they were all locked.

Suddenly, she came upon a table made of glass. There was a bottle with the label "DRINK ME" and a tiny golden key beside it. She picked up the key. Alice drank every drop in the bottle and felt herself growing smaller and smaller. Now she could go through the

little door which she unlocked into the loveliest garden she had ever seen, with beds of bright flowers and cool fountains.

Alice walked in between the plants which seemed like huge trees to her. She saw a little house in a clearing. The front door was open and she went into the house. She saw a little box full of delicious-looking little cakes.

Alice took a cake and ate it. She grew taller and taller. The rabbit tried to get in but Alice filled the whole house!

So, it became angry and began to throw pebbles at Alice. To her surprise, the pebbles turned into little cakes. Alice ate a cake and found herself growing smaller again.

Alice went out of the rabbit's house and soon found herself in a little wood. She saw a caterpillar sitting on top of a large mushroom. It was smoking a very long pipe.

Alice told the caterpillar how she had changed size from big to small and then to big again after she had followed the rabbit down the rabbit hole.

"Eat one side of the mushroom. It will make you small," the caterpillar said to her. Alice broke off a piece of the mushroom and became smaller.

Alice walked off again. Suddenly, something moved over her head. She looked up at the branch of a very tall tree, and saw a Cheshire Cat. It was grinning at her. Alice asked the Cat which way to go as she wanted to find the White Rabbit she had been following.

The Cat pointed to the path she should take to reach the place where the Hatter lived. "A Hare lives in that direction," said the Cheshire Cat.

Alice hurried away at once.

Alice walked on and soon came to the March Hare's house. Alice saw a table in front of the house. It had been laid for tea. The March Hare and the Mad Hatter were sitting at the table. The March Hare asked Alice to join them for tea. Then, they began a strange conversation. It made no sense at all and Alice got up from the table and walked off.

Alice soon came to a garden where the Queen of Hearts, whose attendants were dressed like playing cards, called her to play croquet with them. Alice had to use a flamingo for a mallet, and a playing card for a wicket, while the ball was a hedgehog! The Queen of Hearts suddenly began shouting "Off with her head!! Off with her head!!!"

Alice was quite puzzled. She bit into the cake which she had taken from the rabbit's house and felt herself growing taller.

"Off with her head! A trial!! A trial!!!" the Queen of Hearts shouted again.

Immediately, her attendants rushed towards Alice. They told her that she was accused of stealing the Queen of Hearts' tarts and that they would hold a trial.

The attendants rushed towards her. At once Alice thought that they were going to attack her and cried out loudly.

Then, she heard a voice she knew so well. "Alice! Wake up! You've been asleep for a long time!" her sister said as she shook the little girl.

"I've had such a strange dream," Alice rubbed her eyes. She told her sister all about her adventures as they walked back home.

✳ ✳ ✳

The Flying Trunk

There once lived a merchant who was so rich that he could have paved the whole street with silver coins. But he was also very careful with his money. So when he died, he left his vast wealth to his son.

Now, the son was the opposite of his father. He lived in great luxury and, instead of saving his father's hard-earned money, he spent it lavishly. At last, he had nothing left.

The young man's friends did not want his company as he was very poor now. But, one of them was kind-hearted. He sent the young man an old trunk with the message to pack up and leave the place.

The young man sat on the trunk and felt very depressed. His hand accidentally touched the lock and a strange thing happened. The trunk began to fly up! It flew through the window and floated up in the sky.

The young man was quite surprised and clutched on tightly in case he fell. The trunk flew over many countries, rivers and mountains, over lands which were very cold or very hot. The people below looked like tiny busy ants as they walked about!

At last, the trunk came to an eastern land. It landed gently. The young man hid the trunk beneath

a pile of dry leaves and went to see the Sultan at the Court.

The young man was dazzled by the great golden throne set with glittering jewels. A man with a long beard sat on it. It was the Sultan.

The young man was amazed by the wealthy Sultan. He began to boast about his own wealth, and told the Sultan all about his travels which took him to many countries.

The Sultan's beautiful dark haired and dark-eyed daughter was also present in the Court. She was enchanted by the many stories which the young man told them. And soon, she fell in love with the young man who was quite handsome to look at. He too fell in love with her and promised to take her to the distant lands he had told her about.

Soon, the Princess told her father, the Sultan, that she wished to marry the young man. He did not give his permission right away and hesitated a little. But the Princess pleaded with her father so earnestly that at last he agreed.

The beautiful Princess was always present when the young man told his wonderful stories about distant places - lands which were so cold that one had to dress in warm clothes. This was unusual for these people who lived in a warm place.

He told them how differently these people lived, how they worked for a living and what they ate.

In the meantime, preparations for the grand wedding celebrations went on. Splendid silk and satin gowns were stitched for the Princess. Gold and silver ornaments and precious jewellery was also specially made for her. The whole city was illuminated. Buns and cakes were given to the people.

There was great excitement everywhere. For the people thought that their Princess would be marrying a very wealthy man who had great powers too.

The Sultan ordered that there should be a grand display of fireworks.

Soon the time of the wedding came. The young man went to make sure that his trunk was safe. But where was it? The trunk was burnt! A spark from a firework had fallen on it and had caught fire. Now there was nothing left but ashes.

The young man's dreams were also in ashes now. For he could no longer marry beautiful dark-eyed dark-haired Princess. He was only a poor man. How could he hope to marry a rich Sultan's daughter?

The young man quietly left the palace and went away from the country.

The beautiful Princess waited in vain for him to come and cried bitterly.

The young man wandered around from place to place sadly. He had wasted his immense wealth and had now lost his chance for happiness. He was also very shabbily dressed and had to beg for food. He told his stories to whoever would listen, often in exchange for a meal or a loaf of bread. His face would wear a sad look when he described the wealthy Sultan of an eastern land and his beautiful dark-haired dark-eyed daughter.

Then, he would move on to the next town in search of some happiness.

❋ ❋ ❋

Puss in Boots

Once upon a time there lived a miller. He died and left all that he owned to his three sons. He was not very rich and had only three things to leave. They were: his mill, his ass and his cat.

The eldest son took the mill. The second son got the ass. This left the cat for the youngest son.

He looked at the cat and sighed.

"My brothers will be able to earn a living," he said loudly. "But what can I do with just a cat?"

The cat heard what the youngest son said. He said to his new master, "Don't worry, master! Just make me a suit of clothes and have a pair of boots made for me too. If you give me a sack, I will begin my work soon."

The youngest son was quite surprised for he did not know what the cat planned to do. But the cat got what he had asked for. He wore his new clothes and put the hat with the plume on his head. He wore his fine new boots and took the sack.

He looked very grand now. So his master called him "PUSS IN BOOTS."

Puss in Boots went to a meadow where many rabbits lived. The cat saw a fat rabbit run into the sack. He quickly closed up the mouth of the sack and went to the King and said, with a bow, "Your Majesty,

my master, the Marquis of Carabas, has sent you this rabbit."

"Thank him for the gift," the King said, though he had never heard of the Marquis of Carabas. It was a name which Puss in Boots had made up.

For the next three months, Puss in Boots caught something every day and presented it to the King. He always said that the gift had been sent by the Marquis of Carabas. The King grew very impressed.

One day, Puss in Boots heard that the King would be going for a drive in his carriage by the stream with his beautiful daughter. He told his master to go for a swim in the stream. The young man did as Puss said. While he was in the water, Puss hid his torn old clothes.

Just as the King's carriage came into view, Puss shouted loudly," Help! Help! My master, the Marquis of Carabas is drowning!"

The King ordered his footmen to help the Marquis. Puss told the King that someone had stolen his master's clothes. So, the King ordered a fine set of clothes to be brought from his castle.

The young man looked very handsome in the fine clothes. So, the Princess fell in love with him at once. The King noted that and invited the Marquis to join the royal party in the carriage.

Puss in Boots ran ahead of the royal carriage and told the workers in the fields he passed by to tell the King that they belonged to the Marquis of Carabas. He frightened them and they agreed at once. When the King passed by, he asked the workers to whom the fields belonged and heard that the owner was the Marquis of Carabas. He thought that the Marquis would make a fine rich husband for his daughter. In the meantime, Puss came to a huge castle. It belonged to a rich giant who really owned the fields the King had seen. Puss had found out the kind of magic the Giant could do. So, now he asked if he could speak to the owner of the castle.

The servents took Puss to a huge hall where the Giant sat.

Puss bowed respectfully and said, "I have just learned that you can do wonderful things which no one else can do, that you can change yourself by magic into any animal, like an elephant, a lion or a tiger. Is it true?"

"Of course it is true!" the Giant replied. "I can change into any kind of animal by magic."

"I challenge you to show me!" Puss said.

The Giant changed into a lion. Puss was quite frightened to see the fierce lion in front of him. Then the Giant changed into his real form once again.

"What a great fright I had? You looked like a real fierce lion!" Puss said to the Giant who looked pleased when he heard the praise.

"You can change by magic into a big animal," Puss said. "But can you change yourself into a tiny creature, like a mouse, for instance?"

"I'll show you!" the Giant roared.

He changed himself into a mouse and ran across the floor. Puss sprang at him at once and ate it up! That was the end of the Giant!

The King's carriage came to the castle just then. He wanted to see it. Puss welcomed the King and the Princess to the Marquis of Carabas' castle.

"What a very fine castle you have, Marquis!" the King exclaimed.

He wished to go in. The Marquis led them to a great hall where a grand feast had been laid. It had really been laid for the Giant and his friends! After the feast, the King said that he would like the Marquis to become his son-in-law.

The Princess and the Marquis were glad to hear the King's words.

And so, the two of them were married. Puss in Boots had served his master faithfully. He lived with The Marquis of Carabas and the Princess happily for the rest of his life.

✳✳   ✳✳   ✳✳

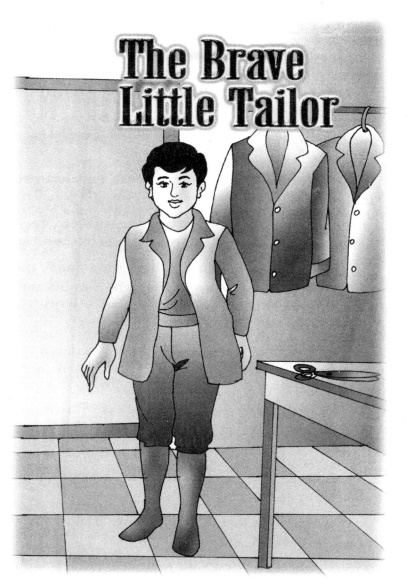

It was a fine sunny morning. A little tailor was busy cutting out a waistcoat from a cloth. Suddenly, he heard a woman call out, "Cakes for sale! Who'll buy my fresh cakes?"

"Come here!" the tailor called out. "I will buy a cake!"

He chose a small cake which had pink icing on top.

"I will finish cutting out this waistcoat and eat it later," the tailor thought and put the cake on the table.

The smell of the cake spread throughout the room. It attracted a swarm of flies who flew down to sit on the sugar icing. The tailor was very angry. He picked up a cloth and beat at the flies with it.

The little tailor stopped at last and counted the number of flies which had been killed. There were seven dead flies.

"Well, seven is a good number," the little tailor looked pleased with himself. "Seven at a blow I have killed!"

He grew more and more proud as he thought about his deed.

"It is a great feat. The whole world must know of it!" he decided.

The tailor quickly cut out a belt, hemmed it and stitched in large capitals : "SEVEN AT A BLOW."

The tailor fastened the belt around his waist and decided to travel forth into the world. His workshop seemed too small now after his valiant deed.

Every where the tailor went, the people stopped and stared in awe. They read the words on his belt and whispered admiringly to each other.

"He must be a mighty warrior," they said and nodded their heads. They then went to tell their King about him.

The King sent one of his courtiers to bring the little tailor to the Court.

The tailor was pleased when he heard that the King wanted to see him. He went with the courtier.

"Will you join my army?" the King asked.

"I am ready to serve you, Your Majesty," the tailor replied.

Soon the King sent for the little tailor and told him that in a forest in his Kingdom, there lived two fierce giants. They created fear and caused much damage.

"If you can kill the two giants, I will give you my daughter in marriage as well as half of my Kingdom," the King said.

"I shall bring the giants to you so that you can see how brave I am," said the little tailor. "You can take the army with you," said the King. "Nay. I shall do it alone, for I have killed SEVEN AT A BLOW! But the army can come with me and stay at a distance," the tailor replied.

The tailor marched in front of the Royal Army. He stopped when they all reached the forest and told the men to stay there while he went to kill the giants.

The tailor had made his plans carefully. He filled his pockets with stones and climbed up the tree under which the two giants were sleeping. They were snoring so loudly that the branches above them shook!

The tailor crept along to a branch so that he sat just above the sleeping giants. From that position, he flung down one stone after another on the chest of a giant.

The giant did not stir for some time. The tailor flung stones again and the giant woke up. "Why are you punching me?" he shook his companion.

"You must be dreaming! I did not touch you at all!" his friend replied and they both went back to sleep.

After some time, the tailor threw bigger and heavier stones on the first giant. He roared angrily as he was hurt and began fighting with the other

giant. The tailor watched from above as both of them fell unconscious.

The tailor came down the tree and tied up the two giants securely. He then called the army to help him to take the two giants to the King.

The little tailor and the army took the two captive giants to the Court so that the King could see them himself. The King was very impressed by the tailor's feat.

But before he gave the promised reward, he had another task for the tailor.

"Before the wedding, you must capture a wild boar which has caused much damage in the forest," said the King.

Once again the little tailor set out for the forest.

This time too he told the army to stay far away before he captured the boar.

When the boar caught sight of the tailor, it ran at him with foaming mouth and gnashing tusks. But the little tailor nimbly stepped out of the way at the last minute and the boar ran into a tree. Its tusks became firmly caught in the trunk.

The tailor quickly tied a stout rope around the beast's legs and called the army to take the boar to the King.

This time the King could not hold back the reward. He still did not know that the little man was only a tailor.

The wedding was a grand affair. The Princess grew to like her husband and learned that good qualities like courage, kindness, and cleverness were more important in life.

❊❊   ❊❊   ❊❊

The Emperor's New Clothes

Many many years ago, there lived an Emperor who was more fond of new clothes than anything else in the whole world. In fact, he paid more attention to his clothes and spent all his money on new clothes and finery. He did not bother about anything else which took place in his kingdom. He had a coat for every hour of the day. And, because he spent so much time changing his dress, his people did not say "The King is in Court". They said "The King is in his wardrobe"!

The Emperor's Capital was a beautiful city with gardens and parks. Soon, word spread about the Emperor's love of new clothes and many merchants came to sell costly silks, velvets, laces, satins, gold and silver ornaments. They had made these specially for the Emperor.

The Emperor was always ready to see such people. Other important matters were forgotten as the Emperor discussed the quality of the materials shown to him, the kind of things he wanted or the jewellery he desired to be made.

One day, two impostors arrived in the Capital and went to see the Emperor. They said that they were weavers. They claimed that they could weave the most beautiful cloth ever seen. It would be fit only for the Emperor. The marvellous quality of this

cloth was that it would be invisible to anyone who was stupid or unfit for the position he held.

The Emperor at once wanted to have a splendid suit of clothes made from the material. He also wanted to find out which of his ministers was stupid.

The two impostors took the Emperor's measurements and promised to begin work at once. The Emperor gave them much gold in advance.

The Emperor also gave them special rooms so that they could work undisturbed. The two impostors set up their looms and pretended to be working hard, but there was really nothing on the looms.

After some days, the Emperor decided to go and see the cloth which the weavers had made. But he first sent two ministers ahead of him. They could see nothing on the looms, but pretended that the cloth was marvellous. The Emperor entered the room.

"Why, there is nothing on the looms! Am I so stupid and unfit to be an Emperor?" the Emperor thought and pretended to be pleased. The ministers urged the Emperor to wear the new clothes for the grand procession which was about to take place.

On the day of the procession, the two impostors told the Emperor to stand before the mirror.

"Will Your Imperial Majesty remove your outer clothes so that we can help you to wear the new

clothes?" they asked respectfully. The Emperor took off his clothes and stood in his underwear. The two impostors pretended to hand him the new clothes one by one. They smoothed down an imaginary cloth on his body and pretended to tie a train.

The Emperor turned and twisted before the mirror and pretended to admire the new clothes.

Soon, the Lord of the Court arrived to help the Emperor. They pretended to hold the train and the procession began. The two impostors went to their own rooms and packed all the gold and silver which the Emperor had given to them. Then, they quietly left the city and ran far-away to another place. They were not to be seen again in the Emperor's kingdom.

The procession was a very grand affair. The people lined the streets to see the Emperor's new clothes about which they had heard so much. Many people stood at their windows to see the procession pass. They were really eager to know if they or their neighbours were stupid! The Emperor sat astride his horse and smiled and waved to the people.

The people nodded their heads with approval and said, so that their neighbours could hear, "The Emperor's new clothes are really grand. Look at the beautiful train!"

"Yes, the material is very fine too" others agreed.

No one dared to say that he saw nothing or it would prove that he was stupid and unfit for whatever position he held!

Suddenly, a little child said loudly, "Why! The Emperor only has his underwear on!" The people began whispering the same thing. The Emperor knew that the little child was right and in his innocence had said the truth. He changed from that day and no longer spent so much time on clothes, but began to rule properly instead.

❄❄   ❄❄   ❄❄

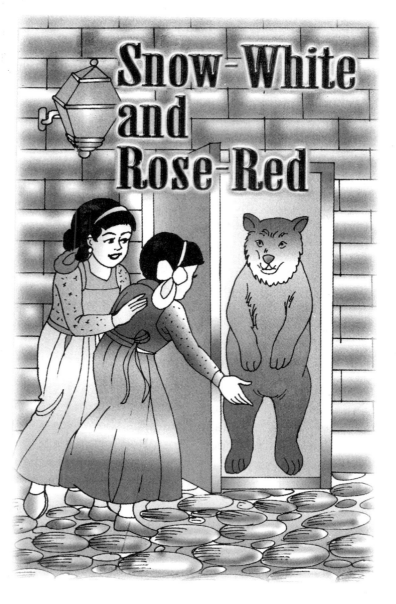

Snow-White and Rose-Red

Once upon a time, there was a poor widow who lived in a little cottage near the wood with her two daughters. They were called Snow-White and Rose-Red because they were like the snow-white roses and the red roses which bloomed on the two rose bushes which grew before the cottage.

Snow-White and Rose-Red were good and happy children. They loved being together and played with the little rabbits and deer near their cottage without any fear. They helped their mother with all the work, and also helped her to keep the cottage neat and tidy.

In the evening, when all the housework was done, Snow-White and Rose-Red would sit by the fireside with their mother. She would read from a book and the two girls would listen to her. Or they would all sit with darning and stitching. Snow-White and Rose-Red had learnt how to sew from their mother.

One winter evening, as they sat by the fireside with the snowflakes falling outside, there was a soft knock on the front door. "Rose-Red, go quickly and see who it is. Perhaps it is some traveller outside who wants shelter from the snow," said her mother.

So, Rose-Red rose from her chair and went to open the front door thinking that there was some poor man caught in the snowstorm.

Instead, a great brown bear poked his shaggy head in! Rose-Red shrieked with fright and ran far-away from the door. Snow-White hid behind her mother's chair.

"Don't be scared. I'm freezing with cold and want to stay by the fireside. I will go away soon," the bear said.

The widow and her daughters lost their fear and asked the bear to stay with them in the cottage during the cold winter. When spring came and the days became more warm, the bear left the cottage as he had promised. Snow-White and Rose-Red were sorry to see him go away.

Some time later, their mother sent Snow-White and Rose-Red to gather ripe berries. They came upon an old dwarf whose long white beard was caught in a split of a log of wood.

Snow-White and Rose-Red tried with all their strength to free the dwarf with little success. Finally, Snow-White took a pair of scissors from her pocket and snipped off the beard which had been caught.

As soon as he was free, the dwarf marched off grumbling that they had hurt him and had cut off his beautiful beard.

The next day as they were walking, they heard a cry for help. A large bird had caught the dwarf between its claws and was flying off with him. Snow-White and Rose-Red frightened the bird with sticks so that it dropped the dwarf and flew off.

Once again, the dwarf did not thank the girls for helping him and marched off. When the girls were picking flowers in the wood, they saw the dwarf again. He had spread a large sack of precious stones on the ground and thought that no one had seen him. The sparkling stones so attracted the attention of Snow-White and Rose-Red that they stopped their work to admire them. The dwarf looked up suddenly and saw the two girls. "Why are you two staring like that? Haven't you ever seen precious jewels before?" he shouted. "Go away! You are nosy girls!"

Just then there was a loud growl and a huge brown bear came lumbering out of the wood. The dwarf was terrified and tried to run away before the bear caught him.

"Spare me, my dear Lord Bear! I will give you all my wealth. But please give me my life! I will give you anything you want, but please let me go!" the dwarf begged.

The bear growled angrily in reply and came nearer and nearer.

The bear knocked the dwarf with his paw so that he fell on the ground.

Snow-White and Rose-Red were scared and were going to run away, but the bear said, "Snow-White and Rose-Red, don't be scared. Wait for me, I will go with you too!"

They recognised the voice and stopped. When the bear came up to them his brown hairy coat suddenly fell off and there stood a tall handsome Prince, dressed all in gold. At his feet lay the bearskin! "I am a King's son," he said. "I was hunting in the wood one day and was caught by this wicked old dwarf!"

"Then what happened?" the girls asked. "The dwarf stole all my treasures and cursed me to roam as a brown bear till his death freed me. Now he is dead and I have become a Prince once more," he said.

They all went to the cottage and told the mother all that had happened. Snow-White married the Prince and Rose-Red married his brother. They all went to the palace to live. The two rose bushes which grew in front of the cottage were taken to the palace and planted there. They bore beautiful snow-white and rose-red roses.

❋❋   ❋❋   ❋❋

The Wild Swans

Once upon a time, there lived in a northern land a King and Queen. They had twelve children – eleven sons and a daughter who was called Elisa. The Queen died when the Princes and the Princess were very young children. So, the King decided to marry again. Then the Princes and the Princess would have a mother to look after them, he thought.

But the new Queen did not like the eleven Princes and Princess Elisa. She was also jealous of the great love the King had for his children. She herself had no children.

The new Queen had special magic powers. One day, she saw that the eleven Princes and Princess Elisa playing in the garden and cast a spell which would turn them all into wild swans. The Queen heard a loud flapping of wings and rushed to the window of her chamber. She saw eleven white wild swans flying by, and wondered where the twelfth wild swan was.

She did not know that Princess Elisa had escaped the wicked spell which the Queen had cast. For she had been playing in another part of the castle.

Princess Elisa was scared that her stepmother would cast another wicked spell on her. So, she ran far away and hid in another country.

"I wish I could find my brothers one day!" she cried as she sat beside the sea shore.

Princess Elisa had wandered all day in search of her eleven brothers. So, she was very tired and lay down to sleep. Just when the sun was about to set, Elisa saw eleven white wild swans flying towards the land from the sea. The sun sank below the water and suddenly the swans' white feathers fell off. And there stood eleven handsome Princes with gold crowns on their heads – Elisa's brothers.

Princess Elisa called out their names as she saw her brothers and hugged them joyfully. They too recognised their sister. Soon, they learned how cruelly their stepmother had treated them all.

"How can I free you from the wicked spell?" Princess Elisa asked. She wept sadly when she thought of her brothers who had been changed into wild swans.

"We must first take you far away where the Queen cannot find us. We have a plan and must work soon. We can have our human forms only when the sun sets. When it rises every morning, we are changed into wild swans again," the eldest brother said to his sister before he was changed back into a wild swan at daybreak.

The eleven swans were back the next evening after the sun had set. They brought many reeds which they wove into a hammock. Elisa sat on the hammock and the eleven Princes who became wild swans at

daybreak the next morning, flew up in the air with her.

The swans were very careful with the hammock when they flew over the sea. One of them shielded her from the sun's rays. After flying for hours, they set the hammock down gently in a forest which was very far away.

"Goodbye, dear sister!" they said before they left. "Do not be sad. The spell will be broken soon!"

As they flew away, a sweet voice told Elisa that her brothers' words were true and that the Queen's wicked spell would be broken soon.

Elisa saw a beautiful fairy who gave a bundle of stinging nettles and told her to make eleven coats with long sleeves. "You must not utter a single word while you are making them. Throw the coats over the wild swans and they will be changed to Princes once again," said the fairy.

Princess Elisa was very happy when she heard what the fairy said. She worked day and night to make eleven coats with long sleeves and did not mind when the stinging nettles hurt her hands. She neither sang nor laughed even once. One day, the King of the country came riding by. He saw Elisa working and fell in love with the beautiful girl who spoke not a word when he asked her who she was. He took her

to his castle on his horse. Elisa was dressed in fine silks and jewels. But she never spoke a single word and continued to make the coats from the stinging nettles.

In the meantime, the wicked stepmother came to learn that Princess Elisa was living in a far-off country whose King wished to marry her. She travelled the distance to see the King and warned him that the girl who never spoke was really weaving plans which would harm him.

"Put her to death!" she said.

Princess Elisa could not defend herself as she was determined to be silent till she finished making all the eleven coats which would free her brothers.

The King kept her in a tower where she worked on the coats day and night. Princess Elisa's brothers, the wild swans, visited her often and begged her to speak, but she never uttered a word.

The wicked Queen persuaded the King to delay no more and have Elisa put to death at once.

As she was being taken through the streets, her brothers, the eleven wild swans flew down. The nettle coats were finished, except for one sleeve of a coat. But Elisa flung them on the swans. Immediately, her eleven brothers stood before her. The spell of the

wicked Queen was broken. But the youngest Prince had a swan's wing as the sleeve had not been finished in time.

Now Princess Elisa told the King all that had happened to her and her eleven brothers. He begged her to forgive and marry him. The wicked Queen lost all her evil powers and was banished. The wedding of Princess Elisa and the King was celebrated grandly and they all lived happily ever after.

Rapunzel

Many years ago, there lived a man and his wife who longed for a child. At last their wish was going to come true and they were very happy.

The cottage next to their own cottage had a beautiful garden with many flowers, fruit trees and vegetable plants. But no one dared to enter the garden as it belonged to a wicked witch.

The wife looked out of her window one day and saw plenty of rampion (a kind of herb) growing in the witch's garden. It looked so fresh and green that she wanted to eat some.

She pointed it out to her husband and begged him to get some rampion from the witch's garden.

The man wanted to please his wife. So, at night he climbed over the wall and plucked some rampion from the witch's garden. His wife cooked and ate it. She soon longed for more rampion and begged her husband to steal it from the witch's garden again. So, once more he climbed over the garden wall at night. But this time he was caught by the witch.

"How dare you steal my rampion!" she cried angrily.

The man begged her to forgive him as his wife wanted to eat rampion. He also told the witch that his wife was expecting a baby and would die if she

could not eat some rampion! "All right. I will let you go. You can take as much rampion as you want every day. But on one condition: you must give the baby to me when it is born!" the witch said.

In his fear, the man agreed to the witch's condition and she let him go. Time passed and a beautiful baby girl was born to the wife. They were very happy. Then, the witch appeared and took away the baby with her.

"Please spare our baby!" the wife begged. "The child belongs to me now. I will look after her and bring her up like my own child," the witch replied and went away with the baby.

She named the baby girl RAPUNZEL which was another name for the rampion which grew in her garden.

Rapunzel grew up to be a very beautiful child. She loved to play in the garden. Often when she saw the man and his wife who lived next door, standing at their window watching her play, she would wave to them. But, she did not know who they were and wondered why they looked so sad.

Rapunzel grew lovelier and lovelier day by day. Her golden hair grew very long. She made two braids which were as thick as ropes!

Rapunzel was such a pretty girl that the witch feared that many young men would want to marry her. So, she shut her up in a tower. It had no staircase or door, but only a little window high up in the wall. When the witch wanted to enter the tower, she came and stood outside the tower and would call, "Rapunzel, Rapunzel, let down your hair!"

Then the wicked witch would climb up the two golden plaits which Rapunzel let down to the ground.

One day the King's son rode by. He heared someone singing a lovely song and stopped to listen. It was Rapunzel singing in her lonely tower.

The Prince looked up and saw Rapunzel at the window.

The Prince was quite surprised to see all this. He decided that he would also climb up and find out more about the lovely girl who lived in the tower.

The Prince waited till the witch went away. Then, he went close to the building and called out softly, "Rapunzel, Rapunzel, let down your hair!"

Rapunzel was also quite surprised but she let out her long golden plaits. The Prince then climbed up to meet her. They both fell in love with each other.

One day, the witch came to learn that the Prince visited Rapunzel every day. In a fit of rage, she seized Rapunzel's long golden plaits and cut them off.

When the Prince came as usual, he called "Rapunzel, Rapunzel, let down your hair!" He climbed up the plaits which were let down at once and was horrified to find the wicked witch in the tower room.

The Prince drew his sword. The witch moved away but tripped and fell out of the window down to the ground far below.

Rapunzel and the Prince never saw the wicked witch again.

The Prince had brought a ladder with him. Rapunzel and the Prince climbed down the ladder and rode to the Prince's castle. There was great rejoicing in the kingdom as the wedding preparations began.

The people loved the beautiful girl who would soon marry their handsome Prince. They were also very glad that the wicked witch was dead at last.

When Rapunzel learned about her true parents, she asked the Prince to let them live with them all in the castle.

Rapunzel's golden hair grew long again. She looked very beautiful and ruled as a good Queen with the Prince when he became the King.

※ ※ ※

Beauty and The Beast

Once upon a time, there lived a merchant who had five daughters. The youngest of them all, who was called Beauty, was the prettiest. The merchant had been very rich but had lost all his ships at sea. So, he had to live in a small cottage. The elder sisters were quite selfish and grumbled about the change in their lives. They made Beauty do all the work in the cottage. But Beauty liked to keep the small cottage very clean and look after her father. She sang happily as she did the work and arranged fresh flowers in the vases everyday.

One day, the merchant received news that one of his ships, which he had thought had been lost, had come to port. The merchant and his daughters were very happy. The merchant had to go to the port to take charge of the ship.

"What shall I bring back for you?" he asked each of his daughters.

The elder sisters wanted costly velvet, silk and satin clothes as well as jewels. The merchant then looked at Beauty and asked her what she wanted.

"I really do not want anything. But since you have asked, I would like you to bring me a rose", Beauty replied.

The merchant agreed and set off on his horse for the port.

But when the merchant reached the port after nearly two days, he learned that his ship had been sunk at sea by pirates. He was as poor as he had been when he had set out from the cottage!

The merchant set out on his journey back to the cottage. Soon a great storm sprang up and he lost his way. But he saw a huge castle and made his way towards it.

He passed a beautiful garden and some fountains in the courtyard. But there was no sign of anyone.

The tired merchant entered a large room where a table had been laid for a splendid meal. He waited for some time but no one came. So, he began eating heartily. Soon he felt tired and saw a comfortable bed in another room and lay down on it to sleep soundly.

The merchant awoke the next morning and found that breakfast had been laid on the table in the front room. But still, there was no sign of anyone. The merchant ate and went out into the beautiful garden. He saw a rose bush covered with beautiful roses and remembered Beauty's words. So, he stretched out a hand and plucked a rose. At once he heard a fearful loud roar and looked around. The merchant trembled with fright when he saw a great Beast which came towards him.

"You ungrateful man! I gave you food and shelter.

But in return, you are stealing a flower from my garden!" the Beast growled angrily.

"Please forgive me for plucking the rose! It is for my daughter", the merchant said as he fell on his knees before the Beast.

The merchant was frightened at the Beast's anger.

"Please spare my life. I will give you anything you want from me!" the merchant begged. "So, you have daughters! All right, I will let you go if you send me one of your daughters to live here with me in this castle after three months!" said the Beast.

The merchant could do nothing but agree to the Beast's condition. The Beast then gave the merchant all kinds of costly gifts to take home. The merchant was greeted by his daughters. The elder sisters were very happy when they saw the costly things their father had brought. Only Beauty saw the sad look on his face and asked him what the matter was. The merchant told them all about his adventures in the Beast's castle and the condition the Beast had laid down.

At once Beauty decided to go. And, after three months, she went to the Beast's castle.

At the Beast's castle, Beauty found a beautiful room ready for her. She had splendid clothes to wear

and good food to eat. Beauty liked to read and found many books in a room. So, she led a comfortable life.

Beauty was scared of the Beast at first, but she grew to like him for his gentle ways. He always sat with her when she ate supper and always asked her to marry him. But Beauty always said "No!". One night she had a strange dream that she saw a reflection of her sick father in a magic mirror. Beauty asked the Beast the next day if she could go home.

"I know that you will stay back and I will surely die!" the Beast said sadly.

"No! I promise that I will come back after a week", Beauty replied.

The Beast gave Beauty a magic ring which took her in a minute to her father's cottage. The merchant was very happy to see Beauty and recovered after a few days. Her elder sisters were jealous to hear about Beauty's comfortable life in the Beast's castle and pretended to be sad when the time came for her to return after a week. So, Beauty stayed on for another week. But she missed the Beast very much.

One night she had a dream that the Beast was dying. She took the magic ring which transported her to the Beast's castle. She found the Beast almost dead and cried bitterly.

"Don't die, dear Beast! I love you too much and will marry you. So, please get well soon!" Beauty cried.

At once the Beast disappeared and in his place stood a handsome young Prince. He told Beauty that one day a wicked witch had cast a spell on him and that he had to become an ugly fearful beast. The spell would be broken only when a beautiful girl agreed to marry him as a beast. Beauty was filled with great happiness as the Prince led her to the castle. Her father and her elder sisters came to live with them. They soon changed their ways and became good daughters. Beauty and the Prince were soon married and lived happily ever after.